For Alex
Enjoy your ... with

Natural Mindfulness

Your personal guide to the healing power of Nature Connection

Written by
Ian Banyard

Photoart by
Miyuki Miura

VISION MAKER PRESS

1

ISBN 978-1-9995849-2-4

First Published July 2018

Imprint - Ian Banyard

Designed, Printed & Published by Vision Maker Press

Printed in Great Britain by www.visionmakerpress.com

Front cover photograph credit Melanie Magdalena

CONTENTS

Dedication

I would like to dedicate this book to my children: Joseph, Sophie, Molly and Lacey. *May you always be a part of Nature and may Nature always be a part of you.*

Acknowledgements

This book would never have been written and published without the help and support of some very special people. Firstly, I'd like to thank my wonderful wife Penny for her belief in me and her patience and tolerance of a man who loves to wander off for hours into Nature and then spend hours writing about it.

Secondly, I couldn't have produced this book without the talent and guidance of my publishers, Naz Ahsun and Sarah Ray of Vision Maker Press.

Finally, I'd like to thank all the people who share my love of walking mindfully in Nature, the guides, our walking members and all the other writers, practitioners and scientists who are passionate about promoting *Nature Connection* and the benefits to our health & wellbeing it can provide.

Foreword

Nature gives rise to all life, including our own. Our bodies and minds originated in the natural world and are made up of Nature's elements. We are Nature and part of something much greater than ourselves: the wonderful awe-inspiring web of life!

Many of us have forgotten this undeniable truth and live our lives as if we are separate from Nature. With the evolution of our wonderfully creative mind and our incredible ability for conscious abstract thought, we spend more time dreaming up theories, concepts and belief systems than paying attention to our direct experience. Simultaneously, our lives have become increasingly urban and spent indoors. Neglecting our innate bond with Nature is the cause of much of the suffering in our world – in fact, 'Nature Deficit Disorder' is contributing to an epidemic of unhappiness and the current global environmental crisis.

It's time to bring our awareness back to the natural world. Firstly, experiencing Nature will make us happier – science has proved it. Secondly, practising mindfulness in Nature will make us wiser. The natural world holds one of life's greatest truths – that our wellbeing is intimately linked with that of the rest of Nature, so what we do to Nature we do to ourselves.

This leads to the third reason to restore our innate bond with the natural world. People protect what they love, and a true love of Nature will inspire solutions to the creation of a more sustainable world.

I hope you enjoy your journey with *Natural Mindfulness* as did I when I joined Ian on a *Cotswold Natural Mindfulness* walk. I felt inspired to experience the natural world, to love it, share it and care for it with all my heart and mind.

CLAIRE THOMPSON Author of *Mindfulness & the Natural World* and *The Art of Mindful Birdwatching*

My Story

"Natural Mindfulness is my pathway to finding, healing, knowing, and releasing my true nature" – Ian Banyard

Some of my earliest memories are of being outdoors playing in the natural world. I've never felt vulnerable or afraid in the wilderness. For me, being lost in the woods or immersed in Nature feels very natural. In Nature, I feel I am home.

I was born in 1961 and grew up in Gloucestershire, a beautiful part of the UK. My mother was a free-spirit and my father was a sensitive dreamer. They both shared a love of Nature and wildlife. There were no computers, tablets or smart phones to occupy our minds and attention, and only three channels to watch on the television. Sometimes with friends, more often alone, I would lose myself for hours wandering and playing through meadows and woodland in search of the peace and freedom that was often missing in my day-to-day life.

Like my parents, I was a sensitive, free-spirited dreamer who felt emotions deeply. As I grew, I tried to hide them. Our family was good at hiding our private life from the outside world. Mum's free-spirit was diagnosed as mental illness, a condition still stigmatised and misunderstood today, but even more so in the 60s and 70s.

Growing up with a mentally ill parent is very challenging - emotionally, psychologically and financially. When things became too much for me, I would flee to my bedroom or head out into the local woods in search of peace and some solace. On cold, wet days I would sit at my window gazing across the back gardens at my favourite pine tree in the distance. In my mind I would climb right to the top and sit in the cradle of strong branches. Hidden and sheltered among the pine needles and cones, I'd imagine looking down on my world from a different perspective. On warmer, drier days I would set off into the wilderness and lose myself for hours absorbed in the wonders of Nature. My sanctuary.

School days were also an escape from home life, but they brought different challenges. I attended a traditional all-boys' grammar school, where strict rules and corporal punishment enforced discipline. My sensitivity and love of the natural world meant I would get upset when other boys hurt and damaged Nature. Seeing my distress only seemed to encourage them to do it more, as it meant the opportunity to hurt me too. I eventually learned to harden and didn't appear to get upset as much. But I would often secretly return to the scenes of their crimes against Nature to try and repair the damage done and rescue the creatures they had harmed.

The other challenge I had at school was learning. Being a daydreamer, I found sitting attentively in class for long hours difficult. If my mind wasn't stimulated, my attention would drift. From my classroom window I could see a hill in the distance across the river, with a wild and open landmark crowned by a row of tall trees. My teacher often caught me staring out of the window at those trees instead of concentrating on his lesson; he would get annoyed with me for not paying attention. My school days were a kind of *school daze*. I am now aware that I used daydreaming to easily and naturally escape from a world I had little or no control over. In a nature-induced daydream I felt safe, relaxed and my mind was free to explore. I felt like me. I had found, although I didn't realise it then, *Natural Mindfulness*.

According to Florence Williams in her wonderful book, *The*

Nature Fix, this is *the holy grail* of brain states. Apparently, zen masters, surfers and great poets, tap into it too. More commonly known as the *calm alert zone*, this state of mind shows up as alpha waves in the brain that can be measured. When the brain is in an alpha state, we are both relaxed and alert at the same time. It is often referred to as *flow* or *bliss*. Athletes call it being in the *zone*, meditators often call it *being at one with the universe* and it is even gaining in popularity in the world of business and health as *mindfulness*. There are numerous courses, classes, books and even apps available on the market to help you be more mindful in life, all promising to boost your creativity, health and wellbeing. Being able to access this brain state is the key to a type of natural, peak performance.

I am sure we have all experienced times when our body is relaxed, our mind is alert, our awareness increases, and our consciousness seems to expand with a sense of awe. Sadly, for most people, this flow state is quite rare and can be fleeting. Yet this state seems to happen quite easily and naturally when we encounter the beauty of the natural world.

Back to my story.

After leaving school, like most people, I was encouraged to get a job and earn money. I got married and we bought a house. We both worked hard to pay our bills. We had a baby boy, then a baby girl and then another baby girl. So, we moved to a bigger house. We got a larger mortgage. We worked harder, sacrificing our needs for the needs of our growing family. The next ten years ticked by and I had grown numb. I rarely enjoyed time in Nature unless it was with the family. Even when we did pack a picnic and go, we would also pack all the stresses, strains and worries with us too. Eventually, as I approached my forties, it all became too much for me and my life derailed.

All through my early life Nature had been my sanctuary. It gave me the clarity, balance, and the connection that I often felt was missing from my life. I always felt better and re-energised after a spell in the wilderness. As an adult I had lost sight of this. I had also lost touch with my true self; the intuitive and instinctive parts of my nature. I had been programmed, like many people, to live in a manufactured world and look for logical and rational solutions for emotional and psychological life problems. When I failed, my instinct took over and I fled, back to Nature, in search of my true self.

For the next five years I hid from life immersed in one of the UK's most beautiful Natural Parks, The Lake District in Cumbria. During this time, I began to reconnect with my love of Nature, walking on the fells, around the lakes, in the forests and along the shoreline, exploring the landscape around me. I also explored my inner landscape; the one full of memories, thoughts, feelings, experiences and insights. At times during these years of reclusion, I experienced anger, bitterness, guilt, shame, deep sadness and depression. I also experienced moments of a profound sense of inner balance, healing and intimate connection with the plants, animals and landscapes around me. The beauty and tranquillity of the natural world stimulated my senses and expanded my awareness. This meditative state of being would come effortlessly to me. It felt natural to be this way when I walked mindfully in Nature. Over time and many miles, the darker days began to fade, and I would experience more of these moments of *Natural Mindfulness.*

I practised purposefully, bringing my attention to the landscape around me and using my senses to guide my mind. I'd intentionally move my focus between panoramic vistas to tiny details like the veins on a leaf, or the way the sunlight danced on the surface of a lake. I would stand still in the forest with my eyes closed, allowing my other senses to flourish: hearing, feeling and smelling more than I would notice when my eyes were open.

In the Summer and early Autumn/Fall, I would gather fruit, berries and nuts as I walked and enjoy practising 'mindful eating'. The best way to do this, I discovered, was to look at what I was about to eat while resisting the urge to just pop it in my mouth and chew. I would then smell to see if I could detect any fragrance and notice what effect that had on my thoughts about eating it. The best bit was holding the berry or nut in my mouth while resisting the natural urge to chew and swallow, allowing my taste-buds to help me experience all the subtle flavours. Having chosen to swallow, I tried to follow the sensation of the food from my mouth, down my throat towards my stomach, just to see how long I could be aware of the food.

The combination of walking with mindfulness in a natural environment gave me a clarity of thought with which to contemplate the most important questions in my life. On my daily walks I would frequently receive insights and guidance in the form of metaphorical life-lessons. I discovered that these life-lessons in Nature, were all around me, the more present and tuned into Nature I became.

One day I was walking in a forest, feeling particularly sorry for myself, and contemplating how unfair life could be, when I came across the upturned roots of a fallen tree. As this giant fir tree had crashed to the ground following a storm, it had crushed some smaller trees and saplings beneath its heavy trunk. The tree reminded me of the tree I would gaze at from my bedroom window as a child; I immediately felt bereft for the tree and my lost childhood. As I switched my contemplation from the past to the present moment, I experienced an intuitive insight. I was reminded of the importance of looking after my roots (my values and beliefs) and the importance of grounding them in a strong nourishing soil (my relationships and community). This lesson from Nature reminded me how I was like that tree in the forest. I needed deep roots, a connection to others who shared my beliefs and values. I knew in that moment that it was the lack of these essential elements in my life that had led to my fall. I looked again at the smaller trees and young saplings that had been damaged and crushed by the fallen giant, and tears welled up in my eyes as I thought about the effect my fall had had on those I cared about and loved. I also realised that there might be people who could learn from my experiences and discoveries. People who might be going through what I'd been through. People who might benefit from my guidance. Not long after the discovery of that fallen giant in the forest, I decided it was time to begin my journey back.

In 2006 I returned to the Gloucestershire Cotswolds, an area of outstanding natural beauty. I reconnected with a louder, much busier world, but this time I made sure I got the balance right. I remarried in 2010 and our beautiful daughter arrived a year later.

On a warm and fresh Spring day in 2014 I went for a long wander in Nature looking for answers to this question: *How can I bring the me I am in Nature back into the world?* I had also been reading the work of Joseph Campbell, author of *The Hero with a Thousand Faces* and resonated deeply with what he refers to as finding *our bliss*. Joseph Campbell said, *"If you follow your bliss, you put yourself on a track that has been there for a while waiting for you, and the life you ought to be living, is the one you are living"*. All I needed to do was work out what my *bliss* was.

I had been walking mindfully in Nature for a few hours contemplating Campbell's words and reflecting on my time in the Lake District trying to find and heal myself, when a seed of an idea took root. Over the days, weeks and months that seed turned into a sapling, and I launched my first Natural Mindfulness walk on the 22nd August 2014. A year later and the seed of an idea had stronger roots and started to blossom. People started resonating with what I was doing and wanted to join me on a walk; some felt ready to guide their own Natural Mindfulness walks. So, soon after, I set up *Cotswold Natural Mindfulness* and started training guides and connecting with others in the world who shared my love of *Nature Connection* and mission to help others reconnect. That seed of an idea was now becoming a forest.

At the time of writing this book interest in *Nature Connection* and Wellbeing is rapidly growing, worldwide. A longing for *Nature Connection* is awakening in us and people from all over the world are creating ways to reconnect with Nature, to build nurturing communities and create more sustainable ways to live in the world. *Nature Therapy, Forest Therapy, Shinrin Yoku, Forest Bathing, Ecotherapy, Rewilding and Natural Mindfulness* are just a few of the many ways people are being encouraged to form a new relationship with the natural world.

Science is also helping to confirm what generations of humans have sensed for thousands of years; that forests and natural landscapes heal us. I am part of a global movement of *Forest Friends* that includes scientists, authors, medical practitioners and Nature practitioners who all share my passion. We believe humanity is at the dawn of a large-scale reconnection with Nature, which can transcend previous environmental movements and reshape our world. This undercurrent is gaining momentum and influencing every element of our lives.

Thank you for taking the time to read my story and gain a better understanding of why I have written this book. It took me a long time to remember who I truly am and realise what I have to offer the world. This book is my way of guiding you along your own path to more clarity, better health and a deeper connection with Nature, your true nature and life.

Ian Banyard

A message from Photo-Artist, Miyuki Miura

Hi, it's nice to meet you!

I'm an Inspirational Nature *Photo-Artist*. I call myself a *"Photo-Artist"* not a photographer because I don't feel I'm "taking" pictures. I feel I'm playing in and with Nature and making the beautiful unseen, visible.

When I'm in Nature, I am in a timeless and *physical-sense-full* world, and I feel like I become part of Nature - one with Nature. One of my dreams is to travel all over the world and play in and with Nature wherever I go so that I can share the unseen beauty of Nature and miracles of this world with people like YOU!

I have walked a wonderful, magical life path, although it took quite a long time to find my real path. However, I know now that everything I went through made my life so abundant. I completely believe that Nature pictures can convey the energy of Nature and help us to connect with Nature and ourselves simply because we are part of Nature.

I would love you to know how beautiful your soul is regardless of who you are, what you do or how you think of yourself. Nature is made of love and we are also made of love. When we resonate with our love of Nature, we can feel our true selves.

My sincere wish is:

- May every single person live their own unique life, fully.

- May peace prevail on the beautiful planet Earth.

- I am sending love to you through my pictures.

- May your every single day be filled with love, peace & bliss!

Miyuki Miura

Visit Miyuki Miura's Website to discover more of her wonderful images and inspirational quotes:

www.inspirationalnaturepictures.com

How to Use this Book

I am so pleased that you have joined me and all the other like-hearted and open-minded people who love Nature, enjoy walking and have a positive curiosity for *Natural Mindfulness*. Walking mindfully in Nature is one of the most effortless ways to improve our health and wellbeing. To wander or sit in Nature with all our senses open comes naturally to us. Anyone and everyone can participate and benefit from the walks, exercises and insights in this book.

To get the most benefit from this book It is important for you to complete the full seven days. You are in complete control of the journey. You choose when, where and for how long you walk mindfully in Nature. This is your *unique* programme, your *unique* experience and will ultimately be your *unique* success.

You can walk wherever you choose; ideally in the countryside, a forest, woodland, on a hillside, through fields, country lanes, along a sea-shore, or if you are unable to get away from everyday life, a park, your garden, or even a walk into work can be just as good. The opportunities are limitless, and Nature is all around when we stop to notice.

As I am writing these words in my notebook, I am sitting on a bench in the centre of a town. Tall buildings, busy shoppers and noisy traffic surround me. As I look around and shift my attention, I notice the abundance of Nature which shares this moment and space too. I can hear the birdsong. There's a warm breeze on my face. There are trees coming into bloom and Spring flowers immerging. A small white pigeon feather floats slowly down in front of me, drifting gently on the breeze. The feather lands on the pavement drawing my eye to a new green shoot. The shoot has forced its way out of the darkness through a crack in the pavement. It instinctively grows towards the sunlight, forever reaching for the clear blue sky above me. While sensing the natural world around me, I stop writing; all thoughts of anything other than that present moment stop. I experience an overwhelming feeling of calm, clarity and connection. I am having a *Natural Mindfulness* experience and it feels wonderful. When I return to my writing, everything flows.

Each chapter describes a *Natural Mindfulness* exercise you can practise during each walk. Each exercise is an inner journey. I recommend focussing your attention on the journey rather than get distracted by the destination. Noticing what you experience during the exercise is of greater importance than completing, or successfully achieving it.

Before you are introduced to the seven walks, you will find a chapter all about preparing. The chapter includes what you may need to take and may want to consider before starting each journey. There is guidance on preparing yourself for each walk too. Preparing will ensure you get the most out of your experience.

After each exercise there is an opportunity to focus on your experience. Find a spot in Nature where you can sit quietly (sit-spot) and reflect on your walk.

Each walk also includes a link to an online video to help you more easily understand and learn these simple, yet powerful exercises. These exercises are based on some of the ones I use and practise on my *Cotswold Natural Mindfulness* walks and I feel very excited and honoured to be able to share them with you and a wider audience through this book.

Natural Mindfulness is accessible to everyone, although

some people, for example wheelchair users and those with visual or hearing impairment, may need to adapt some of the exercises. This book is ideal for people waking up to the realisation that positive change in the world starts from within and starts with us. Each walk introduces a simple yet powerful *Natural Mindfulness* exercise that guides you closer towards a more connected life. A life connected to Nature, a life better connected to other people, communities and a life connected to yourself and your own unique *true nature*.

The seven walks outlined in this book include stunning and beautiful photographic images of Nature captured by accomplished inspirational Nature Photo-Artist *Miyuki Miura*. Each photograph contains a unique, intuitive and insightful message bestowed to you from Nature via Miyuki with love and gratitude. After each exercise I encourage you to seek out a quiet sit-spot where you are unlikely to be disturbed, so you can meditate, contemplate, or gently focus on these images, quotes and your own experience. There are journal pages with each exercise too that will enable you to record your thoughts, feelings and any insights that come up during your reflections.

On your return from each walk, I invite you to share your experience. Sharing is a great way to increase our understanding and knowledge of experiences. Sharing *Natural Mindfulness* experiences is also a wonderful way to guide and help others. You can do this in several ways. Sharing with family and friends directly. You might like to invite them along on a walk and show them what you have been doing. Sharing on social media; it is a great way to share posts, photos and videos of your experiences. There are several Facebook Groups associated with *Natural Mindfulness* and *Nature Connection* you can join and share with. Or you can set up your own. You can also share with your local communities too by considering guiding walks yourself. There are details at the back of this book and some useful online links.

Walking the path is much more enlightening than merely knowing the path exists. You could just read this book and still get value from it, but if you want more, I urge you to take it with you into Nature and turn the knowledge contained in the pages into understanding, wisdom and action.

To support your ongoing journey, I have included a chapter on the healing power of Nature, which includes information on some of the latest scientific studies and findings. There is also further information about joining my *Natural Mindfulness Community* and links to other *Nature Connection* organisations, practitioners and resources you might find useful.

What is Natural Mindfulness?

When you describe something as natural it can mean different things. Natural can mean existing in or derived from Nature; not man-made or manufactured. It can mean in accordance with the nature of someone or something. A person having an innate talent for a task or activity is often referred to as *a natural*.

Mindfulness is a translation of an ancient word to describe the quality of being conscious or being aware of something. Mindfulness is a mental state achieved by focusing your awareness on the present moment, while calmly acknowledging and accepting your feelings, thoughts and bodily sensations.

Natural Mindfulness

The term *Natural Mindfulness* is simply a description for the activity of walking mindfully in Nature. At a much deeper level it could be described as the awareness of the fundamental nature of our being, reality and existence for life.

Rather than prescribe what *Natural Mindfulness* 'is', I prefer to share with you what it could be.

Natural Mindfulness could be a way to reconnect with the natural environment in a mindful way and remember that we are part of the natural world and not apart from it. There is evidence that suggests our ancestors believed it was important to live in harmony with the natural world and they understood the benefit of maintaining a balance. It appears that we may have forgotten this vital connection.

In an age where the prevailing worldview is that Nature is a commodity that we can dominate and exploit, perhaps being more mindful of the natural world and our connection to it is more important now than ever before.

Natural Mindfulness could be a route to improved health and wellbeing. New scientific studies in the medicinal and therapeutic benefits of walking in Nature have revealed that it has a significant, positive impact on stress, mood and even our immune system. Brain scanning has revealed how the natural world via our five senses can enhance positive brain function, lifting our mood, and stimulating the production of brain chemicals such as Serotonin. At a time, here in the UK, when 1 in 4 people has a mental health issue, it's beginning to look like Nature could be a *Natural* anti-depressant. *Mindfulness* – being aware of how our thoughts, feelings and bodily experiences impact on our health and wellbeing – is increasingly gaining popularity. *Mindfulness Based Cognitive Therapy* MBCT and *Mindfulness Based Stress Reduction* MBSR, are proving to be powerful tools to help prevent relapse in depression and the after-effects of trauma.

So perhaps combining the healing power of *Natural* spaces with *Mindfulness* practice – *Natural Mindfulness* - could be the antidote to many of the health issues associated with modern-day living.

Natural Mindfulness could also be a pathway to finding, healing, knowing and releasing our true nature. For many people, there comes a time in life when dissatisfaction creeps up on them. Most of us grow up in a world where our lives come pre-prepared, or pre-packaged based on certain expectations from our families, culture and society. We are expected to go to school, get a job, get married, have a family, keep working hard to help our children get a good start in life, and then retire. Hopefully, with enough invested to enjoy our twilight years, we can watch our children and, perhaps, our grandchildren go through the same thing. I'm not saying we shouldn't do this and I'm not suggesting there is anything wrong with this life. However, what I know from experience is that deep within some people is an urge to explore an alternative life path. Perhaps a life that resonates in a different way to the one based on the expectations of others. A life more in tune with something deep within us – a knowing, an *inner whisper*, a sense that we have an unfulfilled element to our being that is being ignored, suppressed or has been long forgotten.

This growing dissatisfaction can often lead to us embarking on a journey of self-discovery. So, welcome to the start of your *Natural Mindfulness* journey, a simple, yet powerful approach to a deeper connection with Nature and your true nature.

Preparing for Your Journey

Look where your heart leads and just walk one step at a time.

Preparation is an important part of any *Natural Mindfulness* walk. Some positive forethought can ensure you avoid some of the risks of being out in Nature and focus your attention on the rewards it can bring too. Focussing on preparing for your walk is also an excellent way to start directing your mind with a useful purpose.

Here are some of the basic requirements I always share with my *Cotswold Natural Mindfulness* walkers to ensure they have a safe, enjoyable and insightful experience:

Footwear - Walking in Nature means being prepared for varied landscapes and changeable weather conditions. Consider the pathways you will be walking on and check weather forecasts to help you decide on the most appropriate footwear. If you are walking in a park with dry firm pathways, trainers or sturdy shoes will probably be fine. Safety and your comfort is the key consideration. I always pack my walking boots just in case.

Clothing - As well as choosing the most appropriate footwear, it is also useful to consider your clothing. The temperature and conditions during a nature walk can change quickly and so appropriate layers of clothing are recommended based on the local forecasts. Waterproofs, if wet weather is forecast, and appropriate head covering if there is a likelihood of either a hot, sunny day or very cold and wet conditions. During winter months, good socks and gloves are advisable as you will be walking more slowly than usual and stopping at regular intervals to do exercises. In the winter months, I always take a pair of sodium acetate hand/pocket warmers with me to provide instant heat if necessary.

Fluid & Snacks - It is important to always remain hydrated during the walk, so I recommend taking some water on hot days and longer walks. However, be aware that in Nature there are rarely public toilets along the route. On colder days perhaps take some hot water in a flask and your favourite herbal tea bags. On longer walks take a favourite small snack too. These can provide you with a wonderful opportunity to take a comfortable break and introduce the sense of taste more safely into your mindful practice *(see walk 4)*.

Focus - Adopting a specific intention to connect with Nature and yourself in a healing way is an important element of a *Natural Mindfulness* walk. Each walk is designed to help you move through the landscape in ways that cultivate presence, opening all the senses and actively communicating with the landscape.

Patience - Resist the urge to rush. The primary goal is not exercise or physical exertion. The introductory walks in this book should rarely be more than a mile and last between 20 minutes and an hour. It's not about how far you can travel, it's more about being present and enjoying the journey. Walking mindfully in Nature helps us to slow down our busy lives and open the senses, allowing the natural world to penetrate our consciousness more deeply.

Mindfulness - Generously give your attention as you walk and carry out each exercise, or series of exercises as guided. Notice when your mind drifts or becomes distracted and gently bring your attention back to the exercise and the present moment with kindness. It's as simple as that.

Practice - These walks and exercises are not a one-off event. Developing a meaningful relationship with yourself and Nature occurs over time. It is wonderful to return repeatedly to this practice, knowing we are refreshing ourselves and developing mastery. Practising throughout the natural cycles of the seasons, witnessing the beauty of seasonal changes in Nature and noticing the changes in yourself are just a few of the many rewards you can expect to experience while completing the walks and exercises in this book.

Walk 1 - Staying in Breath

*Feel the sparkles
bubbling up inside you.
Let them come out.*

Welcome to the first *Natural Mindfulness* walk and exercise on this seven-day journey. On this first walk you will discover how to connect to the present moment by gently directing your focus to your breathing. *Staying in Breath* throughout your walk will become your access point, or *gateway,* to the present moment. In the present moment, you can then develop the natural state of connectedness I call *Natural Mindfulness.*

Before you start your first walk, it might be helpful to consider and remind yourselves why breathing is so important to your health and wellbeing. *Staying in breath* is not as easy as it sounds. How often when you are out walking do you find yourself *out of breath*, or feel like you've *lost your breath*?

A few years ago, I noticed that I was getting breathless after exerting myself; Sometimes having to stop on a steep climb to 'catch my breath'. I mentioned my concern to a walking friend one day. He laughed and said, 'you need to slow down and stop rushing about like a twenty-something'. On my next few walks I reflected on what my friend had said and gradually became more mindful of the speed I walked; slowing down when I noticed my breathing beginning to labour and quickening my step when the going was easier. I also practiced consciously focussing my attention on the quality of my breaths. The more aware I became the easier it was for me to regulate my breathing. Over the following months I no longer experienced breathlessness and became skilled at *staying in breath*.

Most of us don't think twice about our breathing because it's automatic and we all do it on average 20,000 times a day. When we breathe we are providing our bodies with the oxygen it needs to remain fit and healthy. Unlike fats and fluids, oxygen cannot be stored in the body and must be replenished continuously and steadily, so it is important to know how to breathe well. Oxygen also allows the brain to work and when oxygen is scarce, the blood in our bodies must flow faster. Breathing enables the body to release waste products and toxins. Poor or ineffective breathing can allow these toxins to easily stagnate in our bodies and cause damage. Medical research suggests that most of us use only a third of the actual breathing capacity available to us and don't breathe as well as we could.

Breathing is also the link between our body and our mind. For both to function well, they need oxygen. Our emotional state can have an impact on our breathing. For example:

- Short quick breathing is often associated with a nervous and agitated mind.

- Irregular breathing is sometimes associated with an anxious and disturbed mind.

- Deep, calm breathing is quite often associated with a clear and relaxed mind.

Understanding the importance of breathing and improving the way we breathe can be an effective way of dealing with pain, controlling emotions like anger or fear and keeping a clear and sharp mind.

When our breathing is deep, slow and regular our mind has a better chance of reaching a state of tranquillity and calm. Breathing deeply and slowly can instantly calm us down mentally, as well as physically. Being consciously aware of our breathing at any moment also helps us to live in the present and feel alive. Have you ever noticed how often your mind is thinking about something while your body is doing something else? For example, when driving or getting ready for work, or eating lunch or doing chores? When this happens our mind and our body are not unified.

This simple *Staying in Breath* exercise is designed to help you get your mind and body working together, so both are focused on the same thing.

Exercise 1: Staying in Breath

The aim of this first exercise on day one is to establish a simple way to focus the busy mind on one specific purpose and quickly train it to help you learn an easy and quick way to connect with the present moment. This is a very powerful process hidden beneath a cover of simplicity, just like Nature.

While walking in a beautiful natural environment, take a moment to count your breaths. As you breathe in, count *One* (to yourself) and as you breathe out, count *Two*.

Then as you breathe in again, count *Three* and as you breathe out again, count *Four*.

Do this until you reach *Ten,* then go back to *One* again.

I find it is easier to begin by perhaps standing still or even sitting down, at first. Just until you get the hang of it. Remember, it is quite normal for you to lose count as the mind wanders off distracted by all the sights and sounds around you, or random thoughts you may have on the inside. When this happens, I encourage you to gently bring your attention back to your breathing, with kindness, and start again. Count *One* on the in-breath, then *Two* on the out-breath and so on, until you either lose count again, or finish the exercise.

The purpose of this exercise is not to complete it easily and perfectly. In fact, if you do manage to complete it easily I suggest you stretch yourself by increasing the challenge. I have some favourite ways of increasing the challenge for myself and invite those of you who like a challenge to try them out for yourselves:

1. On reaching a count of *Ten* return to *One* and start over again as many times as you wish. Don't be surprised if your mind wanders and you find yourself counting *Eleven* or *Twelve*, instead of returning to *One*. Again, if this happens, kindly move your attention back to

your breathing and start again from *One*. Losing track is all part of the mindfulness exercise.

2. Increase the number of breaths from *Ten* to *Fifteen*, or even *Twenty*. I like to mix them up to try and catch myself out.

3. Rather than stand or sit still, try walking around in Nature while counting your breaths.

Staying in breath can be both an enjoyable and, at times, an infuriating exercise depending on your state of mind. Please remember that if you are getting agitated with this and any of these exercises, be kind to yourself, stop the practice and simply enjoy walking in Nature.

As you improve your focus on staying in breath you may also like to try choosing your breath. We often take great care over choosing a meal in a restaurant and choosing a drink in a bar or coffee shop. But how often do you stop to think about choosing your breath? There are so many lovely fragrances in Nature such as the scent from flowers and blossoms, wild garlic and herbs. *Petrichor* is the earthy scent produced when rain falls on dry soil. The word comes from two Greek words *petra* which means "stone" and *ichor* that describes the fluid that flows in the veins of the gods. Scientists have recently discovered antibiotic properties in this distinctive fungal aroma found in damp forest soil. I love the fresh smell of *petrichor* in a forest and often choose to breathe it in when I practice breathing exercises.

Once you have chosen your breath, focus on holding on to it for a moment, savouring the fresh, healthy air. Again, just as you enjoy tasting your food and drink, enjoy savouring the air you are breathing. I remember to feel grateful for every breath I choose. It reminds me that Nature, through the trees and plants, is constantly producing this life-enhancing gift. Being mindful of this and appreciating it brings an added quality to this breathing exercise.

Finally, when you feel the urge to breathe out again, slowly release the air back out into the atmosphere. Notice how holding your breath can feel like holding onto thoughts and feelings. There is a gradual build-up of pressure in the body and an instinctive need for release. I sometimes imagine releasing unwanted thoughts, feelings and tension when I release each breath too. I also consider that the breath I release returns to Nature and feeds the trees and plants. Knowing this helps ensure that I always give back more breath than I take. This also adds more quality to the breathing exercise and impacts positively on our health and wellbeing.

Once you have completed the exercise, take a few moments to reflect on it and what you experienced. You can use the journal pages in this book to record your thoughts and feelings, as well as any ideas you get that you can take forward with you on future walks and integrate into your life. You may also wish to meditate, or simply focus on the beautiful image and quote Miyuki has created for this walk too.

When I returned from my five years of isolation in Nature I felt an overwhelming urge to share my experiences. There is a therapeutic benefit associated with talking about and sharing our personal experiences. Perhaps that is why so many celebrities are now writing their biographies? Sharing also helps us to better understand our experiences by re-living the lessons as we share them. Sharing your experiences with others is an important part of this journey too. When we share experiences, we give others an opportunity to increase their understanding and connect with us at a deeper level. Sharing with like-minded and like-hearted family members and friends is the ideal way to do this. If you think this might be difficult for you, I have set up an online Facebook group where you can find others who are walking or have walked a similar journey.

You will find a link to the Facebook group, as well as other online links and resources at the end of the book.

Access the online support video:

https://youtu.be/tvOXdJUmHnl

Mindful Moment #1: We can go days without food and drink if we have to, but only a few minutes without breathing. Yet how much of our daily attention is spent on food and drink compared with an awareness on the precious, life-giving air we breathe? In a world where food and drink is a valuable commodity, it's not surprising that our attention has been hijacked and our mind programmed to focus too much on buying and storing food and drink. It is important to be mindful of the need to have sufficient food and drink available and to plan our mealtimes, however, paying too much attention on future needs can rob us of the present moment. Investing mindful attention on our breathing, while walking in an oxygen rich, natural environment boosts the health of our body and mind.

Breathing
up to 20
Mdd.

Slow down
Notice more
feel breathe flow with
the universe / nature
eb & flow.

didn't find it difficult
as I do breathe work
with yoga classes.
Always feels good to
return to the breath.

JOURNAL

JOURNAL

Walk 2 – Mindful Listening

The time has come...
You don't need to hide
your true nature anymore.
Be free.

Welcome to the second *Natural Mindfulness* walking exercise on this seven-day journey. I hope you found the first *Staying in Breath* experience enjoyable, insightful and useful. Here is another simple exercise that when practised, can be a very useful and effective way to quickly connect you to the present moment.

Listening seems like a natural skill, yet it requires attention and practice to stay present and truly hear what is going on around us. The mind tends to wander, and our internal narratives and busy thoughts interfere with our attention, which can sap our ability to stay focused in the moment. Mindfully walking in Nature provides us with a welcome change of pace. It offers opportunities to listen carefully and redefine how we engage with the natural world around us. The better we are at connecting to the natural world, the better we become at engaging with each other and a busy world. Remembering how to naturally shut out the noise around us and focus our mind on the sounds that bring us joy, enriches our lives. Children naturally do this and can play undisturbed in their inner world, oblivious to the chaos of their parents' world going on around them. When we reconnect to this space of mindful listening I believe we can also connect to an inner, wiser voice, I call my *inner whisper*.

There was a time when my *inner whisper* was drowned out by my thoughts. There is a difference between an everyday thought and an intuitive inner knowing. It's not easy at first to tell the difference. For years, psychologists considered people who referred to hearing voices in their head as insane. No wonder many people keep quiet about what they hear in their heads. They might not even notice they have them. However, if you look carefully at many of the great spiritual leaders, scientists, artists, musicians and social leaders from history, they regularly listened to their inner voices. Perhaps believing that they were hearing an *inner whisper* from their soul.

Today, we refer to these inner voices in terms such as, my *instinct*, my *conscience*, my *intuition*, my *gut feeling* or my *imagination*. Deep down, we sense that these voices are trying to guide us away from dangers and towards opportunities.

In today's busy world, the demands and distractions on our time and attention are greater than they have ever been in human history. Technology has increased at such a rate, bringing us instant, global information at the touch of a screen or button.

We are bombarded with media containing instructions and advice on how to live our lives, what is right for us, good for us, who to trust and what to do. All this noise is drowning out our inner voices, reducing them to a whisper that struggles to be heard over the interference, distraction and misdirection.

Sometimes, in the quieter moments of our lives, we can hear the whisper of our inner voice. We can hear it as we wake, before our mind begins to focus on the day, or just before we fall asleep at night. Often, we might hear it when we are exhausted and want to give up. When we are lost and have experienced too much pain, our *inner whisper* is there patiently waiting for us to hear it. The easiest way to hear our *inner whisper* is to walk mindfully, immersed in the wilderness around you, reconnected with Nature.

When I lived for a time in the English Lake District and walked the Northern Fells, through thick forests and beside beautiful expanses of water, I would hear my own *inner whisper* most clearly. In many ways this inner voice from my true nature saved my life. It gave me hope when I was at low points in my life and guided me once I had the strength to move on.

These days, I find walking along a beautiful shoreline, watching the sun rise and set, is guaranteed to awaken my *inner whisper* too.

Exercise 2 - Mindful Listening Exercise

The aim of this day two exercise is to build on the breathing exercise from day one. It will help you Improve your natural ability to listen mindfully and more easily, as well as help you quickly connect to the natural world around you, and the present moment.

Find a space on your walk and pause. I like to close my eyes to start this exercise, but it isn't necessary.

Take a deep breath in and listen to the sound of the air passing through your nostrils.

Hold your breath just for a few seconds and notice the absence of the sound of your breathing.

Exhale and again listen to the rush of air as it leaves your body until, again, there is an absence of breath sound, then repeat.

Feel free to switch between breathing through your nose and breathing through your mouth. Notice the differences in sound.

After a few breaths, you will be feeling more present and your ears will begin to tune in to the other sounds around you like: birdsong; the wind in the trees; rustling leaves; animals going about their lives. You might hear other sounds like: an aeroplane; passing cars if you're near a road; other walkers, which is fine. All sounds are merely opportunities for you to practise listening, with curiosity and without judgement.

You might notice that your thoughts sometimes interfere with your mindful listening. Your mind drifts off into thoughts about things that aren't anything to do with the sounds around you. When you notice your mind has wandered, just as in the breathing exercise on day one, kindly bring your attention back to listening. Also, resist the urge to judge a sound as good or bad, pleasant or irritating. They are all just sounds. The aim of this exercise is to simply hear them.

Feel free to make natural noises yourself. Stepping on sticks, squelching in muddy puddles, cracking fallen branches, kicking leaves or crunching nutshells. This is a great way to create interesting sounds to hear and have fun with, at the same time. On my Cotswold walks in the Autumn months, we crunch the beech nuts underfoot because the sound and feeling can feel so satisfying. Welcome to Nature's own bubble-wrap!

Once you have completed it, take a few moments to reflect on the exercise and what you experienced. You can use the journal pages in this book to record your thoughts and feelings and any ideas you get that you can take forward with you to future walks and integrate into your life. You may also wish to meditate or simply focus on the beautiful image and quote Miyuki has created for this walk.

Remember sharing your experiences with others is an important part of this journey too.

Access the online support video:

https://youtu.be/inaC08ylhHU

Mindful Moment #2: We are Nature and have a natural self - *our true nature* - and a natural path to follow. Our *true nature* is often changed by the modern world; our *wilder* more *free-spirited* self becomes domesticated by modern living. It's as if we've forgotten we have natural skills that are very real and deep rooted in our essential nature as human beings. The next time you are walking mindfully in Nature, notice your *inner whisper.* Feed it with your attention. Give it priority over your day-to- day thoughts and feelings, noticing what it's telling you and how that connects you to a different kind of feeling. Find other like-minded people you resonate with and share your experiences on a regular basis. Learn to distinguish your inner wisdom from your *outer-tuition.* There is a difference and you will feel it, hear it more and begin to see it all around you.

JOURNAL

JOURNAL

JOURNAL

Walk 3 - Walking Mindfully

Let your gifts shine.

Welcome to the third day of your seven-day journey. On this walk I will introduce you to another simple exercise that builds on the first two exercises. When you have mastered it, you will find it is a very useful and effective way to move mindfully through Nature and quickly connect yourself to the present moment.

Zen Master *Thich Nhat Hanh* is a global spiritual leader, poet and peace activist, revered throughout the world for his powerful teachings and bestselling writings on mindfulness and peace. His key teaching is that, through mindfulness, we can learn to live happily in the present moment—the only way to truly develop peace, both in one's self and in the world.

Through his teachings, I discovered that the everyday act of walking combined with my love of Nature, was an opportunity to recapture the wonder I felt as a child, express my gratitude and create a space – a sanctuary, absent of suffering. The practise of walking mindfully in Nature can release the power and potential of each step to increase our concentration, our insight, and the joy in just being alive.

This simple exercise of focussing on each step is a discipline that is not easy to master at first. It will test your mind because you are probably conditioned to rush from place-to-place. Perhaps you will feel impatience because you want to reach your destination, or slight embarrassment that someone may see you walking at such a slow and deliberate pace.

If you find yourself feeling impatient, a little self-conscious, or you are having thoughts cross your mind you think are negative, realise that these are a positive gift. They are an opportunity for you to practise acknowledging all thoughts and feelings objectively, without judgement or any attachment to the thought or feeling. See how easy it becomes to let these thoughts and feelings go, by practising these *Natural Mindfulness* exercises.

Remember this journey is your journey. You choose the time and place. You choose the space and pace. And if you choose to, you can always switch exercises and experiment with the *Staying in Breath and Mindful Listening exercises from the first two walks.*

Exercise 3 - Walking Mindfully Exercise

The aim of this exercise is to help you slow your mind down by first slowing your body down.

Take a deep breath and as you breathe out take a step forward with your left foot. Move your attention to the foot and notice how it feels as you lift it up and then place it back down.

Then, rather than stride forward with your right as we usually do when we walk, move your right foot forward and alongside your left foot. Again, notice how that feels.

For your next step, switch to moving your right foot first followed by bringing the left forward, then continue to repeat.

Be aware that, at first, you may wobble a bit as your body probably isn't used to walking this way. You might even feel some resistance and an urge to revert to your usual way of walking.

Like with all the exercises in this book, the first few times you do them is more about becoming familiar with a more conscious way of using your body and mind, and will take some getting used too.

As you get more familiar with it, your mind stops telling you *"it's a pointless exercise"*, or *"you're no good at it"* or *"people will see you and think you are weird."* I had these thoughts at first. With a little persistence and practise, it *clicks*. Just like with riding a bike or driving a car, it eventually gets into your *muscle memory* and then you can begin to master it.

Once you have gotten used to walking this way, gently introduce the exercises from the first two days and see how you get along. I find that the whole experience of walking in Nature changes when we walk this way. I notice very subtle changes in light, sound, temperature and even smells. It's a great way to see and hear the wildlife and, most importantly, it is a great way to tackle the urge many of us have to rush through our lives often missing the best bits.

Once you have completed the exercise, take a few moments to reflect on it and what you experienced. You can use the journal pages in this book to record your thoughts and feelings and any ideas you get to take forward with you to future walks and integrate into your life. You may also wish to meditate or simply focus on the beautiful image and quote Miyuki has created for this walk too.

Remember sharing your experiences with others is an important part of this journey.

Access the online support video part 1:

https://youtu.be/IYKvres6A2Q

Access the online support video part 2:

https://youtu.be/XYLBCxdoFBw

Mindful Moment #3: Could there be a connection between the way someone goes through their life and the way they walk along a nature trail? Since launching *Cotswold Natural Mindfulness* in Summer 2014, I have guided hundreds of people mindfully through Nature. I have seen walkers who chatter away often oblivious to what is happening around them and sometimes distracting and frustrating other walkers. Some walk silently with troubled faces, perhaps lost in their thoughts, ideas and worries, occasionally tripping over tree roots, accidently stepping in puddles or snagging themselves on branches and brambles. I have also witnessed walkers who go striding ahead without any idea of where they are going and completely forgetting that the purpose of the walk is the journey and not the destination. Then there are the walkers who think they already *know how* to walk mindfully in Nature and become fixated on doing it the *correct* way. There are also people who walk slowly through the landscape in awe and a sense of relaxed-alertness, completely connected to the environment, each other and their own true nature. All at once.

JOURNAL

JOURNAL

JOURNAL

JOURNAL

Walk 4 – Training Your Senses

Nature has a magical way of expressing its beauty and you are a part of nature.

Firstly, congratulations on reaching over half way through the seven-day programme. By now you have practised three exercises that can help you to access the present moment quickly and easily. The key now is working out how to stay in this moment of *relaxed-alertness.*

This next exercise again builds on *Staying in Breath*, *Mindful Listening*, and *Mindful Walking*, enabling you to start directing your mind in a positive and more nurturing way.

I have always had a fast mind. I can sometimes become overwhelmed with thoughts and ideas, leaving me feeling mentally exhausted. I still recall one summer evening in the 1990s, feeling this way. While driving the long and stressful commute home from a busy day in the office, I decided to take a detour along a quiet country lane, off the beaten track and away from the rat-race. I slowed the car down, opened the windows to feel the warm breeze on my face and breathe in the fresh air. I turned off the radio and tuned into the birdsong. For that brief moment, I felt more relaxed, refreshed and re-energised than I had in a long while. This recollection of a moment when I chose to direct my attention away from stressful thoughts and onto my senses, gave me a feeling of freedom and escape. It is an exercise I will share with you now.

This exercise is a sitting exercise, so remember to take something waterproof to sit on when you prepare for this *Natural Mindfulness* walk. Also, make sure you take a few edible snacks, a drink - perhaps some herbal tea, or collect some edible nuts and berries along the route for the tasting part of this exercise.

The theme of the exercise is *Training Your Senses.* However, unlike physical exercise that needs to be strenuous to build muscles, this exercise is about developing awareness in a gentle way. Because we are often bombarded with visual stimuli and sounds in our busy lives, our senses can become overwhelmed. When this happens, we tend to shut down and limit or block our sensory awareness. Research suggests that we can only focus our attention on around five to seven bits of sensory input at any one time before we get overloaded. When we are tired and stressed it can be even less. After a busy day, it is quite comforting to sit and watch a movie, read a book, cook a nice meal, listen to music or chat with a friend. Most of us settle for one activity as we unwind from our busy day. Imagine trying to do all those things at the same time and you'll get the picture about *sensory overload.*

Our brain has a different area (cortex) for each of our senses. The biggest of these areas is the visual cortex. This means it is much easier for most of us to develop a greater awareness for what we see and be less aware of what we hear, feel, smell and taste. Other animals have different brains and different sensory preferences. Bats and other nocturnal animals have enhanced hearing. Dogs are well known to have an enhanced sense of smell. New-born babies are more aware of touch and feelings until their visual cortex develops and sight takes over. People who are blind or partially sighted often have heightened awareness in their other four senses. They might experience improved hearing, touch sensitivity and are more aware of tastes and smells.

The following exercise will help you become more mindful of your senses and give you an opportunity to bring them more into balance. When we can use all our senses to the best of our ability, in the present moment, I believe we reconnect to a more instinctive and intuitive part of us: Our *true nature.*

Exercise 4 - Training Your Senses Exercise

The aim of this exercise is to increase your focus on sensory awareness in the present moment using a combination of sights, sounds, smells, feelings and taste to connect with the natural world around you.

Find somewhere comfortable to sit where you won't be disturbed and have an opportunity to look out across a landscape or look at a specific object in the distance.

As you sit comfortably, take a deep breath and as you breathe out, gently rest your gaze on an object in the distance and then relax your eyes.

Familiarise yourself with the following script so that you can recall it without having to refer to it on the walk:

Step 1. *"As I am sitting here and looking across this landscape, I am aware that I can also hear..."*. Simply add whatever you hear in that moment. For example, birdsong, the wind in the trees, an aeroplane, whatever you can hear.

Step 2. *"As I am sitting here and looking across this landscape and hearing... I am aware of feeling..."*. This time add in something you can feel. For example, the wind on your face, the ground beneath you, perhaps pick something up and hold it in your hand.

Step 3. *"As I am sitting here and looking across this landscape and hearing... and feeling... I am aware that I can smell..."*. Now add in any smells. If the earth is damp, you might be able to smell the *petrichor,* the earthy scent produced when rain falls on dry soil. Woodland plants like wild garlic are also often easy to detect. Pick up and sniff a piece of bark or moss. Try crushing different leaves between your fingers and notice what they smell like. Sniff your own skin and clothes. You will be surprised by how many different smells are present for you to detect in Nature and wonder how you haven't noticed them before.

Step 4.   *"As I am sitting here and looking across this landscape and hearing... and feeling... and smelling... I am aware that I can taste...".* This is where you get a chance to drink or eat whatever you have chosen to bring with you, or the edible nuts and berries you collected along the way. If you want to enhance the experience, I suggest you include a mindful eating exercise. (I give a description of a mindful eating exercise at the beginning of this book in the My Story section).

Step 5.   Continue this exercise, repeating the sequence of different senses for as long as you wish. Perhaps try experimenting with your different senses and add in a wider variety of things to look at, listen to, feel, taste and smell. And most importantly, enjoy the experience.

Be aware - If at any time during any of these exercises you find your mind wandering, or you begin to worry you might not be doing the exercise correctly, or perhaps get frustrated with yourself, that's normal. It's also a wonderful opportunity to catch your mind wandering and gently bring it back to the exercise. Remember you can stop at any time too. This seven-day programme is your programme to complete at your own pace, in your own space.

Once you have completed the exercise, take a few moments to reflect on it and what you experienced. You can use the journal pages in this book to record your thoughts and feelings and any ideas you get that you can take forward with you to future walks and integrate into your life. You may also wish to meditate or simply focus on the beautiful image and quote

Miyuki has created for this walk too.

Remember sharing your experiences with others is also an important part of this journey.

Access the online support video:

https://youtu.be/TzPo9jyVzjY

Mindful Moment #4: These days most people are aware of the health benefits of training their body. So, they join gyms, classes and groups to build muscle, strengthen bones, stretch, develop flexibility, burn fat and increase blood flow to energise their bodies.

Nearly all of us are aware of the need to develop our minds, by educating ourselves, developing our knowledge, learning new skills and ways of thinking about the world, as well as translating that into our actions and behaviours. BUT how many of us are aware of the benefits of developing our senses? The word to be sensible or rather *"Sense Able"* is a big clue to the importance of developing sensory awareness. Our senses are like super powers that we can develop and extend. ESP – Extra Sensory Perception, or more commonly known as *intuition*, is available to all of us and can be developed just like our bodies and our minds, but it is so much more powerful. Imagine being able to see, hear, feel and sense what others are missing? Imagine being able to distinguish the difference between what you've been taught and what your *intuition* tells you? The more you train your senses, the more present you become and the easier it is to access a state of *Natural Mindfulness.*

JOURNAL

JOURNAL

Walk 5 — Relaxing & Reflecting

*Embrace
your past and
know
you can let it go.*

Day Five is your rest day! This walk is an opportunity to simply walk with no other purpose than to let your mind wander and reflect on your journey so far. Today is about *relaxing & reflecting* on your progress while you walk. There is also nothing stopping you from practising all or any of the previous four exercises: *Staying in Breath, Mindful Listening, Mindful Walking* and *Training Your Senses,* if you wish to.

Before you set out on this walk, I want to draw your attention to a common habit we all possess to different degrees, called *mind-wandering*. Like most things in life, a little *mind-wandering* in moderation is fine and can be very useful for creative thinking and very healthy for us.

Albert Einstein, the most influential physicist of the 20th century and the creator of the general theory of relativity, claimed that his greatest breakthroughs came from a type of creative *mind-wandering*. Einstein would allow his mind to wander as he walked in the countryside to gain inspiration and insights. He would then analyse and test out these leaps in understanding, scientifically, in his laboratory.

Three years ago, I was experiencing growing and persistent feelings of unfulfillment. I was *racking my brain* trying to find an answer and feeling annoyed and frustrated with my inability to do so. On my wife Penny's advice, I put on my walking boots and set out into Nature with no particular purpose or destination. I simply walked allowing my thoughts to wonder while I wandered. During that two-hour walk, I *fell* into a natural state of mindfulness and believe I received an insight - a gift from Nature. That gift was the awareness of *Natural Mindfulness* and the inspiration to want to start sharing it with others.

You might resonate with both those stories and many people have discovered how allowing their mind to wander can help gain clarity and stimulate creative thinking, insights and ideas that solve many of our day-to-day problems. However, *mind-wandering* can also be unhealthy for us, especially when it becomes habitual and self-destructive.

Researchers have discovered other forms of *mind-wandering* that have a negative effect on our health. They also discovered that this type of *mind-wandering* is becoming more common as our lives become busier, more stressful and we rely more on technology.

A recent study using a clever mobile app revealed that on average, for 48% of our day, our mind is not focussed on the present moment. We are literally unaware of what is happening to us and in the world around us for nearly half of our life. This is like walking around for half of your day with your eyes closed, ears covered and no awareness of what your body is feeling. So, if our mind is not on the present moment, where is it?

Well, the research suggests that when our mind is wandering it is focussing on:

- The Past – *thinking about or dwelling on something that has already happened.*

- The Future – *thinking about, planning, worrying or dreaming about something that hasn't happened yet.*

- Nothing – *in a daze, automatically carrying out habitual patterns of everyday behaviour without a thought or purpose.*

While you have been walking and doing the exercises in this book you will have probably noticed that both types of *mind-wandering* have happened. I notice it all the time. I experience both positive and negative *mind-wandering*. However, since practising *Natural Mindfulness* I have found it much easier to pull my attention away from negative *mind-wandering* and purposefully allow my attention to flow as I experience positive and useful *mind-wandering*.

So, today, or whenever you choose to experience your fifth walk, I invite you to walk with a gentle focus. Perhaps reflect on and re-experience what you have been experiencing over the last four walks. If you wish to, revisit the four exercises you have been practising. Do make sure you watch today's video by using the link given at the end of this chapter. It will help you get a much better understanding of negative *mind-wandering*. Then as you walk, dividing your attention between moving mindfully through Nature in the present moment and reflecting on your experiences, simply notice when your mind wanders. When it does, *and it always does*, just gently bring your attention back to the present moment, back on walking, relaxing, reflecting. Always with kindness and a gentle nature.

You may recall this process of bringing your attention gently back to the present moment was what you practised on the first walk (walk one) when you were counting breaths.

As before, when you have completed the exercise, take a few moments to reflect on it and what you experienced. You can use the journal pages in this book to record your thoughts and feelings and any ideas you get that you can take forward with you to future walks and integrate into your life. You may also wish to meditate or simply focus on the beautiful image and quote Miyuki has created for this walk too.

Remember sharing your experiences with others is also an important part of this journey.

Access the online support video:

https://youtu.be/p2gJqsxW6Ag

Mindful Moment #5: It has been estimated that a moment lasts about 3 seconds. This means we each get about 20,000 moments each day. How often do you rush through your morning routines of getting up, washing, getting dressed, eating breakfast, cleaning your teeth, brushing your hair, getting your children ready, applying make-up (or shaving), then driving to work or dropping the kids off? How much of your attention is in the present moment? Have you driven home after a busy day and realised you don't recall part of the journey? Where was your attention? Do you dwell too much on the past, or worry too much about the future and the things outside of your control and influence? Do you spend hours watching irrelevant TV or surfing the internet? How many moments were spent on social media today? These are all examples of the negative *mind-wandering* that robs us of nearly 10,000 moments every day. Your moments are more valuable than money. You can't get them back and there is only a finite number available to you. Being more *Naturally Mindful* in your everyday life can help you pay more attention to your moments so you can relish them, enjoy them, share them and protect them from negative *mind-wandering.*

JOURNAL

JOURNAL

JOURNAL

Walk 6 – Finding the Alive-ness Inside

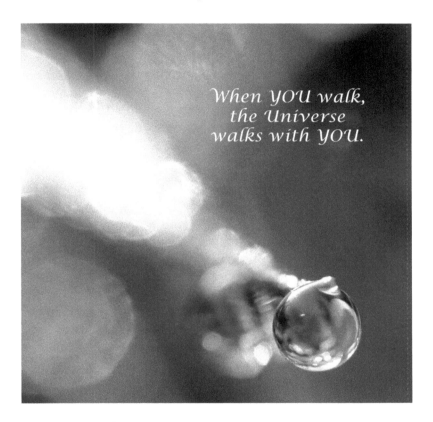

*When YOU walk,
the Universe
walks with YOU.*

Welcome to day six, the most important stage of the journey so far. In this chapter I will share with you what I truly believe is the essence of *Natural Mindfulness*. This exercise, like all the exercises in this book, are simple and very powerful. By practising, you will be able to re-connect to a sense of the *alive-ness* deep inside of you. An *aliveness* that can extend and reach out to synchronise with the *aliveness* of the natural world around you.

Day six is also an important stage of the journey because not everyone makes it this far. In fact, statistics show that only half of us commit to doing something new or different in our lives, and less than 25% of them get this far without giving up.

So, congratulations for getting this far against the odds. I want to really thank you for your commitment to this and to yourself. By choosing to commit yourself to reading this book, then going out and practising the simple, yet powerful exercises proves that you are the kind of person that can get the most out of *Natural Mindfulness.* This book has been written specifically for you.

Natural Mindfulness has purpose. When I walk mindfully in Nature, I naturally connect to the world around me. I hear and see much more of the wildlife and am very aware of the life-force that we share. It could be described as a spiritual experience, a communion or, as I like to think of it, a return to something bigger and more universal than myself. When I am walking in a state of *Natural Mindfulness*, it is as if a part of me, perhaps a more superficial or false version of me, falls away and I become a part of the natural environment. A more natural, real and authentic *me* emerges. The animals and birds appear less threatened by my presence, perhaps regarding me as part of Nature rather than intruding on it. Many creatures in Nature shed their skins or metamorphose as they develop and grow. Walking through Nature with *Natural Mindfulness* feels like a similar process of refreshing and renewing myself.

Everything I have shared with you so far, is designed to help you connect with the natural world around you, using your breathing to calm your thoughts and your senses. What I love most about Nature, is the *'alive-ness'* that we share. Life flows through Nature and flows through us. There is a balance in Nature that exists in us too. There is wisdom and healing available in the natural world that our ancestors were aware of and could easily access. That same wisdom and healing exists today and is easily accessible if only we are *switched on* and open to it.

The following exercise is a pathway to switching yourself on, opening yourself up and inviting the wisdom and healing of Nature in. On my *Cotswold Natural Mindfulness* guided walks, I remind our members that it helps to walk with an open mind, an open heart and an intention to connect with Nature in a healing way. And always enjoy the journey.

Exercise 6 - Finding the Alive-ness Inside Exercise

The aim of this exercise is to connect with the natural world by first connecting with yourself, your own *true nature*. This exercise can be carried out standing still or sitting comfortably as you will be required to close your eyes. Make sure you bring along something waterproof to sit on if the conditions are likely to be wet or damp.

Find a convenient place to stop along your walk where you are unlikely to be disturbed. It is better to do this exercise after you've been walking for a time. As you become aware of your body, such as the muscles in your legs, perhaps notice any change in your breathing and heart rate. Now you are ready.

Close your eyes and ask yourself this question: *"How can I be sure my hand is there if I can't see it?"*

If you feel something touching your hand, make contact with another part of your body or clothing, move your hand away so it is not touching anything and ask the question again. You may feel a gentle breeze on it, or perhaps the warmth of the sun. If you keep searching and focussing your attention on your hand, with your eyes closed, you may begin to notice some sensations from within. You might notice a warmth, tingling, pulsing, or just a sense of something I call your hand's 'aliveness'. It's something that is difficult to describe, therefore often goes unnoticed. On my guided walks, someone might say I feel nothing, but then by focussing on the nothing become aware that there is a something there. An aliveness.

Continue to repeat the exercise, perhaps taking a break to walk on a little more to help generate more aliveness in your body. Once you connect with this feeling you will notice how much easier it gets to reconnect and how quickly it can grow in your awareness.

Once you have a sense of the aliveness in your one hand, repeat the exercise with your other hand, and then with your feet by asking yourself the question: *"How can I be sure my foot is there if I can't see it?"*

As you familiarise yourself with the sensation of *aliveness* in your hands and feet, explore and play with the feeling. See if you can sense aliveness in both your hands at the same time, both your feet at the same time and in both your hands and your feet at the same time.

Notice any differences in the sensations you feel in your hands and feet, be curious. Notice if your mind starts to interfere with thoughts that you aren't sensing what you are *supposed* to be feeling. There is no right or wrong in any of these exercises. Everyone is different and what you sense and feel is right for you. You may not want to call it 'aliveness', if so, call it something else, whatever you like. This is your unique journey, your unique body, your unique experience.

For those of you who feel you've mastered this sense of the *aliveness* in both your hands and feet and want a challenge, you might like to try connecting it all together. Feel the *aliveness* expand into your arms and legs, into your torso, filling your body up with *aliveness*. Some people have said it helps to associate a colour with the *aliveness* so they can feel and visualise it expanding at the same time. Feel free to try that and anything else that helps you connect to your *aliveness*. Remember that you can also use the video link below.

When you have completed the exercise, take a few moments to reflect on it and what you experienced. You can use the journal pages in this book to record your thoughts and feelings and any ideas you get that you can take forward with you to future walks and integrate into your life. You may also wish to meditate or simply focus on the beautiful image and quote Miyuki has created for this walk too.

Remember sharing your experiences with others is also an important part of this journey.

Access the online support video:

https://youtu.be/MQE9_sRP-ZU

Mindful Moment #6: Have you ever considered the relationship between the four seasons of Nature and our own lives?

Spring time is the beginning of new life where we see rapid growth and change in the natural world just like in childhood. It is a time where new-borns begin to take in new sights and sounds and bond with parents. Just as new shoots put down roots and struggle upwards towards the sun. Babies become toddlers and naturally stand, walk and run towards life. There is a freshness to Spring as the Sun, rain, warm air, and cool breeze nourish and stimulate new life and healthy growth; and parents care for their children by feeding them, clothing them, protecting them and loving them.

Summer time represents a joyful and carefree time of life; the brightness of the sky; the heat from the sun; a time of play; to explore; to dream; to look forward and chart new directions. We absorb knowledge as the Earth absorbs the light and water, needed for continued growth; Summer is a time of becoming, of journeying towards an instinctive destination and basking in our beauty, desires and strengths.

Autumn/Fall is the time of reaching mature adulthood; the most colourful season where Nature finally reveals all its majestic beauty as if to say, *"this is what it was all about, this is what I truly am"*. Nature's final flourishing and gradual fall into the deep sleep of Winter – hibernation ensures all the goodness and wisdom accumulated over the year goes back into the ground to nourish the next generation.

Winter time when the world can appear to be a cold, harsh and lonely place, is still full of life. Just because we can't see it doesn't mean that there isn't *'aliveness'* inside the trees and in the soil beneath our feet. Lying dormant below the surface is an abundance of life just waiting for the natural cycle of growth to begin again, the following Spring.

We think of a life as finite and sadly miss too many moments in our seasons. We often race through life towards our playful summers and fruitful autumns, but then try and franticly brake as we find ourselves skidding towards Winter. The key to life is to enjoy as many moments of each season as we can. Enjoy the good and the bad. Knowing that hope is eternal just as the seasons are eternal.

JOURNAL

JOURNAL

JOURNAL

JOURNAL

Walk 7

How to use Natural Mindfulness on Purpose

Nature is made of Love.

Welcome to the seventh and final walk of this series of introductory *Natural Mindfulness* experiences. This final walk in this *Natural Mindfulness* series of seven walks will bring everything you have been learning to mind.

Day seven is about how to use *Natural Mindfulness* on purpose. Being mindful has many benefits; at the very least you can feel relaxed, stress-free and at one with the Universe, which is great! For me, *Natural Mindfulness* has proved to be a very rewarding and useful pathway to discovering and releasing my true nature, enabling me to become a more authentic version of myself. I use the state, *Natural Mindfulness* to help me explore the world around me and within me, as well as empower myself to help others explore their worlds and empower themselves too. That is my PURPOSE.

So, what is the PURPOSE of experiencing and practising *Natural Mindfulness* for you?

There is so much focus these days on setting yourself a goal, an objective, a destination, but how can we truly do this if we don't know who we truly are? It would be like asking a baby where it wants to be in five years' time. That would be ridiculous and yet we continue to ask ourselves this question throughout our lives before knowing *who and where we are?* A friend of mine often reminds his students the simple fact that setting goals and knowing where you want to be in the future is pointless if you have no idea where you are starting your journey from. For example, wanting to be in London and knowing the easiest way to get there all depends on which town you are starting out from and what form of transport you plan to use to get there.

Now you have experienced *Natural Mindfulness* for yourself and have a much better idea of who you are and where you are in your life right now, you can now, perhaps, get a better sense of where you want to journey to. When I walk mindfully in Nature, I often set out with no thought of a destination, I just wander. When I get to a space where the path heads off in different directions and I have a choice of direction, I use the following exercise.

Exercise 7 - How to Use Natural Mindfulness on Purpose Exercise

The aim of this final exercise is to bring all the previous exercises together and provides you with a very useful way to use *Natural Mindfulness,* that serves you and your wellbeing.

As you walk through Nature on this final walk of your introductory journey, set out with no thought of a destination in mind. For this walk it is a good idea to walk in a familiar space where you are happy to just wander around and unlikely to get lost. As you walk, use any or all the previous exercises to help you prepare, get present, expand your senses and synchronise the *aliveness* in you with the *aliveness* all around you. As you become more naturally mindful, consider the thought, or ask yourself the question:

What choices can I make and what actions can I take in my life right now that help me support my happiness, health and success?

How can I be a more authentic version of my true nature?

Then just walk and patiently wait for a thought, a feeling, an insight, perhaps even a sign or a *lesson from Nature* herself.

When I started my own personal journey, there was a lot of noise in my mind, hurt in my heart, pre-conceptions, fears and limiting beliefs that blocked my way and often distracted me from my path. Over the years and with practise I have become more tuned in to my *inner whisper* and use *Natural Mindfulness* to help me make better choices and take actions more aligned to who I truly am, rather than who I think I am.

When you have completed this final exercise take a few moments to reflect on, not only the experience of this exercise, but also the seven walks and your thoughts, feelings and insights about your journey. Please use the journal pages and look back through the journal pages from the previous walks in this book and record any ideas you might have about continuing your *Natural Mindfulness* journey.

Remember to meditate or simply focus on the beautiful image and quote Miyuki has created for this walk too. Perhaps consider creating your own images and quotations from your journey to share with others on our online communities. You can find more information and resources at the end of this book.

Access the online support video:

https://youtu.be/V_iecV345Bs

Mindful Moment #7: Have you noticed how some people are in Nature, but not there? Their body is there, but their mind is focussed on something elsewhere. I see dog walkers preoccupied with controlling the behaviour of their dogs. Parents doing the same with their children. Joggers with headphones on, listening to music and walkers with their heads down texting and taking selfies with a tree. I hear walkers moaning about their work colleagues, their boss, their spouse, the news, the government, the state of the country and what's wrong with the world. All of them infecting the beauty of Nature with the *Manufactured Mindlessness* they create inside their heads. Bringing the world of busy into a place of balance and calm. What if, in the same way that people can infect a Natural space with all the problems in the world, people could also infect all the problems in the world with Nature? I think it's worth finding out and so I challenge you to continue your journey with *Natural Mindfulness,* or any of the Nature Connection practices available, and start spreading the healing power of Nature. And if you don't find an approach that suits you, why not create your own?

JOURNAL

JOURNAL

JOURNAL

The Healing Power of Nature

Nature resonates with the purity in your heart and raises your vibration.

Could Nature be the antidote to today's busy and stressful world?

Congratulations on completing your seven walks and deepening your connection with Nature and your true nature. I want to encourage you to continue your journey and so this chapter includes some of the growing body of evidence supporting the health benefits of walking mindfully in Nature. I have included summaries of studies carried out by scientists as well as anecdotal evidence from people who have personally experienced the healing power of Nature.

There's nothing quite like being deep in a forest or immersed in the natural world. It provides a sense of tranquil awareness and often an escape from what I often refer to as *the world of busy*. The only sounds you hear are those of your own breathing, footsteps, the wind, rustling trees, a nearby stream and the movements of the creatures who call the wilderness home. Sadly, too many of us are too busy to get a chance to experience this. Increasingly people are moving away from Nature into towns and cities. Towns may have beautiful parks but visiting them is often done while doing something else, like eating lunch or checking emails and social media feeds. This is not the same as deeply immersing ourselves in the countryside and studies prove this. Studies also reveal that our health is suffering from time away from Nature and a better balance is recommended.

It is estimated that humans have been around for approximately seven million years and have spent around 99.99% of that time living with Nature in natural environments. Living in towns and cities is a very recent change and the evidence indicates that our minds and bodies are not used to it. We all recognise the sad image of a large animal in captivity continuously pacing up and down. To me, life in the city looks exactly like that. Queues of people moving backwards and forwards to work day in, day out, and then all heading off on their weekend and holiday breaks to try and recharge themselves. We live in a world where we focus more attention and effort recharging our phones, than recharging ourselves. We know our smart phones are only smart when they are plugged into the internet and forget that we are smarter when we are plugged into a more natural environment. Health and wellbeing is all about balance and we are becoming disconnected from the source of our health and wellbeing – Nature.

Over the last 10 to 15 years scientists, mainly in Japan and South Korea, have been accumulating data that reveals some amazing health benefits associated with *Nature Connection*. There is now clear evidence that people who appreciate Nature, and make the effort to spend time in it, are happier, healthier and more creative.

Here is a summary of some of the latest scientific studies followed by some anecdotal evidence from some of my friends who have real-life experiences promoting the healing power of Nature.

Nature is a powerful antidepressant

Studies have shown that walking in Nature, helps to balance levels of feel-good brain chemicals. Levels of oxygen in the brain are connected to levels of serotonin, the neurotransmitter that affects mood. Too much serotonin makes us irritable and tense; too little and we feel depressed. According to scientists, breathing fresh air helps the brain regulate serotonin levels promoting greater happiness and wellbeing. Recent research has also identified a link between forest soil and levels of serotonin. There is harmless bacteria in woodland soil that acts as a natural antidepressant too. This bacterium called *Mycobacterium Vaccae*, can increase the release and metabolism of serotonin in parts of the brain that controls our cognitive functions, our thinking and our mood. Finally, do you remember a parent saying, *'chin up'* when they caught you feeling down? Or recall a sports coach encouraging players to, *'lift your head up'* when they felt they were losing the game? Well new scientific evidence is proving there was something in this too. When we are out in a forest and lift our heads and chins up towards the light and cathedral-like canopy of green trees above us, mood-enhancing brain chemicals are released. Another missed opportunity these days when we have our heads down looking at our phones and other digital devices.

Nature can prevent heart disease, diabetes and obesity

Walking is one of the healthiest activities around. A couple of hours walking mindfully in Nature can burn over 500 calories. It's also much easier on our bodies than running, which puts a lot of pressure on the joints. Walking has been proven to reduce blood pressure and build up levels of fitness, helping to prevent cardio-vascular disease, strengthening our core, improving stability and aiding weight loss.

Nature helps us recover more quickly and feel less pain

Scientists in Pennsylvania proved that just looking at Nature out of your window can have a beneficial effect on wellbeing. A study, in Pennsylvania, was conducted of patients recovering from a procedure to remove their gall bladder. Some were given a room that looked out onto the wall of a building, while others were assigned a room with a view of Nature. The study showed that patients looking at Nature recovered more swiftly and used less painkillers than those whose view looked out onto the wall.

Nature gives the brain downtime to recharge

Our brains use about 20% of all the energy the body produces. This figure can increase by another 10% when we are trying to solve problems. When we sit and rest these days there is a tendency to use our phones, tablets or watch television. Even when we switch off our devices, quite often our minds are consumed by thoughts; often thoughts that worry or annoy us. Our brains need downtime. How often to you find yourself struggling to get to sleep, or find yourself waking up in the early hours? Getting a good night's sleep seems to be getting more difficult.

Recent studies show that in the UK over 50% of us struggle to get to sleep and fail to get enough sleep. Worryingly 75% of those reporting difficulties are women. However, when we are in the daydream state, allowing our minds to wander, the brain can rest and recharge. Scientists have discovered that the brain settles into a default mode where the day-to- day mind chatter switches off. Have you ever caught yourself having driven a familiar route and arriving at your destination with no memory of driving there? This is quite a common condition experienced by all of us at some point in life. Sometimes, the brain needs to switch into this *autopilot* mode to recharge and recover from long periods of over use.

Research has found that dysfunction in this default setting of the brain is present in conditions such as Alzheimer's disease, Schizophrenia and Attention Deficit Hyperactivity Disorder (ADHD). Ongoing research is also looking at ways switching off mind chatter can help those with mental health disorders such as addiction, depression and obsessive-compulsive disorder (OCD) who can have automatic thought patterns that drive repeated, unpleasant behaviour. While the research continues, I suggest you access this state, wandering in Nature, as a safer and easier alternative than driving home in the rush hour.

Nature can lower blood pressure and reduce stress

Stress and stress-related disease costs the UK economy nearly £6.5bn each year, with people taking 10.4 million days off work through stress-related illness. Studies have been carried out in Japan since the 1990s monitoring the effects of a practice I regularly refer to on my *Natural Mindfulness* walks called *Shinrin-yoku,* known in the west as *Forest Bathing.*

Field experiments were carried out in 24 forests across Japan, with 280 participants in total. In each experiment, the scientists would send one half of the participants into the woods, and the other half into the city. The next day, those who spent time in the woods would be sent into the city and vice versa. Scientists found those who spent their day in forests had lower concentrations of the stress hormone cortisol, lower pulse rate and lower blood pressure. In other words, participants were decidedly less stressed when they were in Nature as opposed to an urban environment. Further studies have indicated that when participants were mindful of the health benefits of what they were doing, results would increase by up to 25%.

Nature can boost the immune system

It's not only our minds that benefit from time in the woods, but also our bodies. There is widespread evidence that chemicals emitted by plants, known as *phytoncides,* essential wood oils, can help strengthen the immune systems of humans who are exposed to them. Plants emit *phytoncides* to protect themselves from insects and rotting. A study from the Nippon Medical School in Tokyo found when humans breathe in these chemicals it increases the number of natural kill cells, a type of white blood cell, in our bodies. Natural kill cells are vital to our immune systems as they hunt and kill tumours or infected cells. Again, by adding the element of mindful awareness of the benefits, resulted in further increases.

Nature stimulates our intuition and creativity

Our minds become sharper and more inventive after spending time in Nature. One of the most detrimental aspects of modern society is that we spend far too much time on our phones and digital devices. Whenever we're bored, we unconsciously reach for them. There's a great deal of evidence that boredom helps increase creativity, in the sense that boredom stimulates the creative mind to wander in search of new insights.

A study from researchers at the University of Kansas and University of Utah revealed that spending time in the great outdoors, and away from all the technological distractions, makes us more intuitive and creative. The researchers sent 56 participants on hiking excursions ranging from four to six days in the wildernesses. During this time, the participants were not allowed to use any electronic devices. Ultimately, the researchers found the participants showed a 50% increase in creativity, overall attention and problem-solving abilities after several days in the wilderness, away from technology. Whether this was a direct consequence of exposure to Nature or less technology requires further research for more conclusive evidence. However, this still suggests natural environments stimulate the brain in ways civilisation cannot, improving our cognitive abilities and igniting our imaginations. It comes as no surprise to me how many of history's greatest pieces of art, literature and music were produced by those who truly appreciated Nature and spent much of their time in it.

Nature improves memory

Several studies show that being out in Nature and moving naturally has memory-promoting effects that other walks do not. In a study by the University of Michigan, students were given a brief memory test, then divided into two groups. One group took a walk around an arboretum, and the other took a walk down a city street. When the participants returned and did the test again, those who had walked among trees showed an improvement of almost 20% better than the first time. The group who had taken in city sights instead, did not consistently improve.

Nature can make us less afraid and anxious

When we are afraid we often say, 'I feel nervous'. We are referring to our sympathetic nervous system which controls the *fight-or-flight* response all animals have to a perceived danger. There is another part of our autonomic nervous system called the parasympathetic nervous system which is a much more relaxed 'default' state of being, sometimes referred to as the *digest and rest* response. I referred to this in my story at the beginning of this book when I was writing about *flow* states, *bliss* and *being in the zone*.

An American study discovered that loud noises trigger our sympathetic nervous system flooding our body with a stress hormone called cortisol. Recent studies discovered that this can happen even when participants are sleeping, creating cortisol spikes. The good news is that the study also revealed that sounds found in Nature like birdsong and the running water, can stimulate the parasympathetic nervous system. This can even have a relaxing and calming effect on us when the sounds are recorded. You'll notice these sounds are regularly used in guided meditation, mindfulness practice and other wellbeing activities such as yoga. While I am sitting writing this during Springtime here in the UK, with a publishing deadline, I am surrounded by birdsong coming from the woods that surround my home and feeling remarkably calm and at one with everything.

Indigenous people know, and many of us in Western culture intuitively sense that Nature is good for us. We shouldn't need scientific evidence to prove it. However, in the modern world, many people are so disconnected from the natural world and their connection with it that science is often the best way to convince them to change their lifestyle.

To compliment the science, I also wanted to share with you some anecdotal evidence from those who have already discovered the benefits of *Natural Mindfulness* and *Nature Connection*.

Karen's story

I first met Ian in February 2015. I had been struggling with my mental health and my counsellor suggested I try mindfulness and getting outside for some exercise. I was used to doing meditation but found it difficult to do as a daily practice without guidance. So, I thought I'd give it a go. I arrived for the walk on a very cold February morning, on my own and feeling rather apprehensive. No-one was around. Then I spotted this chap in a high-viz jacket over by the café. That was Ian.

The rest of the group were inside keeping warm – sensible lot! Ian explained all about mindfulness and we did some simple exercises, observations, talked about Nature, walked through the Park and even did some people juggling, which was hilarious!

For those two hours I forgot my apprehension, left my "black dog" in the car and felt great. I really wasn't sure how that happened. Over the following months I joined Ian and other Guides on several walks all over the Cotswolds. At the beginning some of them were physically and mentally challenging. I was physically unfit and had serious mental health challenges. I made a few mistakes like, joining walks when I really wasn't well enough, however was supported by Ian, the Guides and other walkers every step of the way. The metaphors in Nature relate so closely to human experience and I admit, I did shed the odd tear or several. But just getting outside into Nature, leaving behind the regrets of before and worrying about the future in the most beautiful of surroundings was just the tonic I needed. I started noticing things in Nature that I'd just ignored in the past. I walked in all weathers and it didn't matter if it was raining or sunny, cold or hot.

I saw beautiful places in The Cotswolds that I'd never been to, despite living here most of my life. I made new friends, regained my confidence and actually felt quite a lot better. Then Ian said, "You'd make a great Guide Karen, how about it?" My first thought was, "What? Are you kidding?" But he wouldn't give up; so, on January 7 2017 I guided my first walk. I started with 7 people and ended with 7 people – a great result! And I'd got my *mojo* back.

Since then, I've guided regular monthly walks and loved every minute. Connecting with Nature and with people is a great healer. I won't say I'm cured of my illness, it is still part of me, but Nature and mindfulness are just part of my toolkit that keeps me as well as possible.

Lyn's story

Ever since I was a child I have loved to be outdoors. The minute the sun shone I was out in the garden and could while away many hours, poking around flower beds, climbing our one and only tree and picking clovers out of the lawn. This love of the outdoors extended to camping, the smell of the grass, the sound of the rain, new paths to explore.

Then, as I grew older, studying, work, home, children, responsibilities and commitments became the priority. I would still get outside – usually to 'do' something – walk a certain route, run a certain distance, entertain the kids. Then I noticed what Ian was doing and it was subtly different. You know when something is so simple that it needs to be pointed out to you? *Natural Mindfulness* is like that! Ian was walking with a purpose, but it wasn't about an outcome, an achievement or a distraction. It was about being connected with yourself and your surroundings. It was about noticing your body, your breathing, your senses.

When I'm walking mindfully I notice the rhythm of my pace, the cadence of my breathing, the movement or stiffness in my body. As well as an internal focus, there's an external focus of noticing. The expansive freedom, the awesome detail, the varied textures; the smells and sensations of being in a wilder space. The ingredients of a growing, changing, moving environment leads me to connect with myself in a non-thinking, not trying kind of way. It brings me insights without searching for them. There are times when I experience an exciting, blissful surge! When I regularly walk mindfully I find I am calmer and more consistent when I return to the day-to-day activities. By removing myself, I find clarity and focus that wasn't there before.

My British, western culture has taught me that self-motivation and delivering results is what brings success and recognition. This drives action-oriented, outcome focussed behaviours. Not necessarily detrimental behaviours – except all things must come with balance, the best of both worlds. *Natural Mindfulness* enables the polarity of being instead of doing, noticing instead of seeking, understanding instead of problem solving. Having experienced and understood these insights, I will be leading *Natural Mindfulness* walks where I live in Somerset. There's something about the shared experience which can focus your intention when walking mindfully. It's so easy to use the excuse of being busy, or needing to do *x, y and z*, instead of getting outdoors, so having a scheduled date and time means we're more likely to commit to doing it. Do something really simple and effortless for your health and wellbeing and get outside, into Nature and connect to your senses. Become naturally mindful, it's wonderful!

Riina's story

Nature has always been present in my life, in some way. The yard was where I spent countless hours waiting for friends to join me, entertaining myself by digging into the soil, or building snow castles in the winter. Lots of getting bored and "meaningless" poking around in the dirt. In fact, my mother often got frustrated with me and my sister because we showed no interest in Nature. We weren´t interested in learning about different species or helping her pick berries and mushrooms. Instead, we happily ate the berries off the bush while she picked. Most of my childhood memories are connected to Nature and especially summers spent at the summer house (*kesämökki*) or the grandparents farm. There we would shower in the rain under the rain gutter; pick wild strawberries and make a neckless of them on a *timotei* grass, swim and fill our days with endless observing and interaction with the surrounding Nature.

In High school, I started the habit of taking evening walks. I wasn´t into sports, but the dog needed walking. It was also a good time to arrange my thoughts. I would sit at the edge of the lake, dreaming away and writing poems. The teenage experience can be rough. Being bullied, ostracized for one reason or another, Nature became a place where I would return for peace and consolation. In Nature, I found, I was always okay. I was enough. No one judged me, and though I went in there alone or with the family dog, I never felt alone.

As an adult, I realise I am an introvert and that I need a lot of time alone to be able to function properly. I am also an HSP (Highly Sensitive Person) which means I get stressed fast by too many things happening simultaneously, or by too many triggers – sounds, noises and lights in my surroundings. This neural trait is accompanied by the constant doubting and second guessing of myself and the absolute crushing feeling when faced with criticism. Understanding that these are my traits and what they mean for my wellbeing has come only later on in life. Though nothing has changed in my relationship with Nature, I have made it a point to schedule alone-time in Nature. I try to make it to my favorite forest, bi-weekly or at least once a month. But as any parent could tell you, it is not always simple to arrange. But when I start feeling that restlessness building up inside of me, that´s when I need to go.

I wake up early to prepare my coffee and sandwiches. I put on my boots and my backpack. Already, while I am getting ready, I am filled with a joyful expectation - like the anticipation of meeting a dear friend. I know I will feel good. I know I will find peace, calm and a feeling of belonging. And while I am there, I am perfect just the way I am.

John's Story

I first came across *Mindfulness* after the big Anxiety Attack I had in 2012. It was an NHS led course and it really helped me see the world with a more relaxed attitude. Then in 2014 I was in the process of planning my first big personal development event when I heard that Ian was starting something called

Fresh Air Fridays. I jumped at the chance to spend some time with Ian, as I had enjoyed previous conversations and liked the way he looked at the world. However, at the time I was not aware that it was a mindful exercise. Even during that first walk, I don›t recall that we were practising mindfulness. I think this is part of the beauty of doing it in Nature, it's very easy to find yourself being mindful without even recognising that it's what you are doing.

Ian ran through a few exercises on that day, which I STILL use to this day when I teach mental fitness as part of my *Find Your Fire* workshops.

Eventually, Ian changed *Fresh Air Fridays* into *Cotswold Natural Mindfulness* and I became one of the walk leaders. I led my first walk in December 2015 and called my walks the "*Second Saturday Stroll*". I absolutely loved running the walks and it led me to have the confidence to finally put into place my plans to walk the 500-mile pilgrimage across Spain on the Camino de Santiago in April of 2016!

My walk across Spain allowed me many hours of mindful walking on my own, as I was walking around 10-15 miles per day, and even on day 22, I did 37 miles in one day!

It was an immense experience and I am soon to be going back out there to start planning my own walking retreats, which will run for seven days, where the participants will walk around 100 miles in total and, of course, a core part of the retreat will be mindfulness (and meditation) every day.

I have found mindfulness in Nature to be an absolute core part of my new lifestyle and my recovery from depression and anxiety.

An Invitation to Join Me

People protect what they connect to and care about. A true connection with Nature will inspire solutions to the creation of a more sustainable world. And a true connection with ourselves and each other, will provide a healthier way to live in that world. If you have enjoyed your seven-day journey with *Natural Mindfulness* and are feeling inspired to continue along the path, I have an invitation for you.

I would love you to join me in my mission to share *Natural Mindfulness* and *Nature Connection,* worldwide. There are several options available:

1. You can share your experience of the seven-day walks, exercise and insights from your journal in this book and recommend others follow your lead and get a copy of this book too.

2. Join me or one of my guides, on a *Natural Mindfulness* walk here in the Cotswolds. Visit www.naturalmindfulness.uk for further details and to contact me directly.

3. Join and share my online global community with access to worldwide Nature Connection resources. Visit www. natureconnection.world

4. Become a Natural Mindfulness guide yourself and create your own walks, experiences and community anywhere in the world. Visit www.ianbanyard.com and send me an email.

Further Nature Connection Websites

www.naturalmindfulness.uk – Natural Mindfulness UK

www.cotswoldnaturalmindfulness - Natural Mindfulness in Gloucestershire, UK

www.naturalmindfulness.global – Natural Mindfulness Worldwide

http://naturalezayconcienciaplena.blogspot.com/ - Natural Mindfulness in Peru

www.natureconnection.world – A global Nature-based Community linking those seeking nature connection activities with practitioners sharing walks, courses, retreats and experiences.

www.natureandforesttherapy.org – The Association of Nature & Forest Therapy Guides Official Site.

www.foresttherapytoday.com – Finland Forest therapy and home to the International Forest Therapy Days Annual Conference & Retreats.

www.healingforest.org – A global initiative to help people and forests heal through volunteer nature projects.

www.treesisters.org – Promoting collective responsibility for planetary restoration at the grass roots level with a focus on women and tropical reforestation.

www.missionlifeforce.org - A growing international movement of legal Earth Protectors aligning the force of law with the force of life.

Recommended Reading

The Nature Fix – Florence Williams

Forest Bathing – M. Amos Clifford

Mindfulness & the Natural World – Claire Thompson

Shinri-yoku – Prof. Yoshifumi Miyazaki

The Mindful Walker – Alex Strauss

Forest Therapy – Sarah Ivens

Lightning Source UK Ltd.
Milton Keynes UK
UKHW020055060122
396680UK00006B/64